NEAR AT HAND

4-9-93

NEAR AT HAND

Poems by James Whitehead

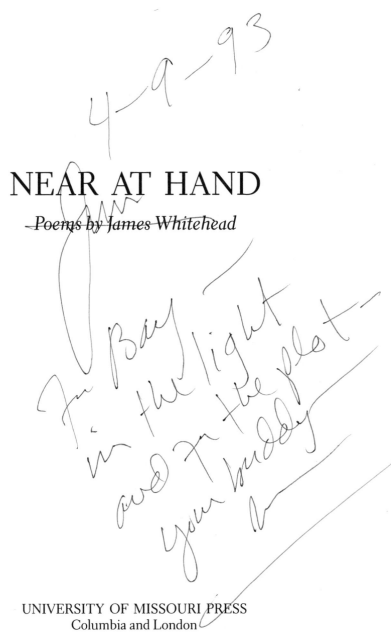

For Bay
in the light
and for the plot—
your buddy

UNIVERSITY OF MISSOURI PRESS
Columbia and London

University of Missouri Press, Columbia, Missouri 65201
Printed and bound in the United States of America
5 4 3 2 1   97 96 95 94 93

Library of Congress Cataloging-in-Publication Data

Whitehead, James.
    Near at hand : poems / by James Whitehead.
        p. cm.
        ISBN 0-8262-0877-0 (alk. paper). — ISBN 0-8262-0878-9
    (pbk. : alk. paper)
        I. Title.
    PS3573.H48N4   1993
    811'.54—dc20   92-36843
                                                              CIP

∞™ This paper meets the minimum requirements of
the American National Standard for Permanence of Paper
for Printed Library Materials, Z39.48, 1984.

These poems—several in somewhat different form—were first published in the
following periodicals: ACM: Another Chicago Magazine, Cimarron Review, Cotton
Boll: Atlanta Review, Cutbank, The Elkhorn Review, The Formalist, Kentucky
Poetry Review, The Laurel Review, The Little Review, The Mississippi Review, New
England Review, The New Orleans Review, Southern Humanities Review, The
Southern Review, and Zone 3. Some of the poems also appeared in Actual Size, a
Trilobite chapbook.

Designer: Kristie Lee
Typesetter: Connell-Zeko Type & Graphics
Printer and binder: Thomson-Shore, Inc.
Typeface: Elante

for Miller Williams,
John DuVal,
and Tom T. Hall

Near at hand is the time when you will be forgetting all;
near, too, all forgetting you.

MARCUS AURELIUS ANTONINUS

Dance on the mountains, shout in the canyons,
swarm in the loose herds like the wild buffalo.

BILLY JOE SHAVER

Contents

ONE

A Natural Theology

Once again a spring has come around
And many of the best I think I know
Are going crazy.
          Light on the warm ground
Is almost God requiring them to grow—
Or, at least, to change—the usual song
And arrogant demand that nature makes
Of moral thoughtful people all gone wrong
So far as they can see.
             Their hands hold rakes.
They comb what later are attractive lawns.
They harrow in their ways, then drive the stakes
Up which flowers and food will climb their dream
Of this one season right.
            They pick up sticks
To make the whole thing work, then plant a tree.
Spring. Spring. They take it personally.

For President Jimmy Carter on His Homecoming
Plains, Georgia, January 20, 1981

People and history begin to say
You were a steward of the earth and cared
For human dignity and knew the dread
Of the awful power that would take away
The good sense of a day of work, and take
Away the night, the night for rest and pleasure.

They have begun to recognize and measure
How carefully you watched the hours strike
Into the future where we live and die,
How carefully you were responsible
And seemed of course to be astonished by
A world outrageous in its vanity,
World unsurprised by greed so terrible
It would desire complete catastrophe.

People and history
Begin to say it's clear you love the earth,
Day in, day out, so much you catch your breath
To imagine how The Death
Might take the possibility of love away.
Thank you, sir, for living with what you know.

Below Is What He Said That Troubles Me

The vanity of things became too clear
When I was sorry that I wasn't asked
To go along to find the suicide,
As he turned out to be.

Our genius died
And friends of his outside myself were blessed
To be the ones who found him lying there,
His eyes open, a thoughtless, drying stare
Expressive of the life he'd felt he'd missed,—
We'd all agree.

They saw him in his blood
And took the seeing for a source of pride,
The perfect homemade horror all have wished,—
For people want this story. All draw near.

Forecast

for our twenty-fifth anniversary and afterwards

Probably if I live I'll end up down there
On the Singing River in a fishing camp.—
The thought of irresponsibility
So quickens my spirits I think I'll cry.

The children, having chosen glory or not,
Will write or come around when they want to,
And Gen, who'll say she's had enough of me,
Will call to check about my heart and weight.—
She'll show up driving the Ambassador.

Well, I'll light up and smile to see her coming.
She always was the best thing that I did,
And the two of us will sit up watching movies,—
And if you think this end is dreams, you're wrong.

With brains and luck all things are possible.

This Is an Elegy for Charlie Harry—
Pilot, Agent, Bounty Hunter, Friend

Lord, if Charlie comes around there,
Say, *Whoah, get down, Charlie!*—
He'll say, *Watch out, Bubbah!*—
Lord, don't take offense—maybe flee
Or take flight, however it is that *you* do it.—
But do not take offense at Charlie Harry.

Lord, you yourself are said to bounty hunt,
After a fashion, letting those go free
You take a fancy to, law or no law,
And also are a master of disguises
The way our Charlie was.

He, at times, for all his playfulness,
Was taken with such powers
As seemed to frighten people.
He frightened people, Lord,
No doubt about it—and you do too—
A billion times more wonderfully for sure,—
Though given a short life in the Deep South
There was little shabby about your Charlie's courage
Or his sense of humor. Lord, you'll love it—
Assuming you really like what you've created
The way Charlie did.

You say, *Get down, Charlie!*
He'll say, *Watch out, Bubbah!*
Then all of us around here will sleep better,
Able to believe in both of you.

Your Slightly Troubled Caudate Sonnet for the Distinguished Journalist Robert Douglas on His Birthday

Somebody better praise these home occasions
Or we'll all stay out in the street full time
Or wander aimlessly in climax forests
Or sulk inside alone, some small decisions
Eating us alive, not worth a dime.—
And at millions of intersections are arrests,
Everything from dents to mutilations,
And in the little valley of no name
A friendly couple fucks with no regrets
During an hour a thousand mothers die,
And fathers, too, things being as they are,
Which has little to do with right or wrong,
Which is somehow a fair biology,
If not the happiest ontology,—

And so we've wisely come in here
To celebrate a proud man who loves the world,
All of the above, hot and cold,
Plus the major political events
That some historians call history,
A man who would edit everything and fear God.

Poem Called Poem

This poem is written in an ancient form—
This poem is old and good for walking with
In a city where girls get robbed to learn
The underground, and how to catch their breath

And go on breathing with a small gun on them.
This poem is loaded, shoots to hurt, not kill,
It is a kind of dope, a little sin
Meant to disarm a woman of her will—

Protects you from the fiends but not from me,
Which is the point of any poem's aim.
I'm in this poem. I am a bad shot, sweet,
But often, like a Gatling gun. Mean mean

Mean. I will give you kisses next time
In a safe place. This poem is an ancient form.

Sestina in Celebration of the Voice of Johnny Cash

with special thanks to Tom Royals and Tom T. Hall—
Fox Hollow, February 25, 1983

Hello, I'm a longtime fan of Johnny Cash and say
By God I love the ways he has to talk or sing
Or somewhere in between,
Whether or not the notes are struck straight on,
Whether or not the tone's exactly play
Or from your basic cold despair.

Back home in Arkansas we've known some cold despair
And know exactly what despair has got to say
About the tune we're just about to play,
And exactly when we have a mind to sing.
We don't refuse our song. We know there's little true
   straight on,
When lives are lived the most part in between.

Most of the time I'm an especial fan of the in between
That never does approve despair.
It halfway laughs and says to carry on—
But not too much. I love to hear Cash say
We all must try to sing
And try, by God, to play.

And then sometimes his songs seem cruel play,
Pretty much straight on and not your in between.
Sometimes when he begins to talk or sing
The whole damn thing is sweet despair,
And life is nothing but the pain he has to say,
And all I want is more of how he carries on.

Lord, sometimes I need to carry on,
Whether or not I've got the right to play,
Whether or not I've anything to say,

And oftentimes I hate the in between,
Raise hell and shoot the chutes to cold despair.
Morning comes with nothing there to sing.
Lord, morning comes and I cry out and try to sing.
FIND A CASH RECORD! PUT THE DAMN THING ON!
THE DUSTY TIMBRE AND THE WATERY PITCH!
  PLAIN DESPAIR!
Hungover or whatever, I mean to play
With the whole wide world that's in between.—
LORD, BLESS EVERYONE WHO HAS A SONG TO SAY.

Exactly. I'm a fan of Johnny Cash, ready to sing or play
What's going on between
Despair and too much fun. That's what I mean to say.

For Ellen after the Publication of Her Stories

You do sunrise as well as anyone
But the dark phone ringing before false dawn
And hours before the actual grey light
Is a mean surprise and no astonishment.—
Hearing it clatter in your dream you fight
As usual to recollect the plot
And know the theme escapes you. You're awake

And you are listening to someone drink
And she is not about your family—
Your sons, parents, brothers, grandchildren
Or any friend or lover at your heart.

She is a lady who will praise your book.
She says she knows you've lived outrageously.
How can you write about such things as happen?
She knows about the night
Of the wildest story, for she was there.
She wasn't. She's nearly crazy with The Fear.
She says no man is fair.
By now you are remembering her life,
While listening to the soft extraordinary sounds of grief.

Pay Attention—
Catch It on the Wing—
Express Some Gratitude—
Don't Question Further

for Pat Grierson

In an old tavern anywhere a song
Gets played by someone troubled by the years
Wherein love sacrificed itself to time,
Got addled by the constancies of fears

And came away not wise but well confused.—
His nearest wife died of a quick disease.
He couldn't understand her lying dead
Or what her mouth had said about their days

And nights before she never spoke again.
He'd never heard her use *sublime* before,
So tied it up with medicine and pain.
Dead, she is terribly both near and far.

The song he'd played was "Ramblin' Man," by Hank.
I said "Sublime," then ordered us a drink.

How It Seemed to Him Away from Home

I'm out of town and visiting old friends,
Old girls and boys of the successful worlds,
And the talk is serious, pretty good
Especially about the things amends
Should be made for: not answering the mail,
Lying through your teeth when the God damned lie
Is obvious, going for the new wife
Of your running buddy, or the husband. Whatever.—

And then some talk about our friends who've died,
Going over names, going for their throats
Long out of sight, drinking and going on
To arguing about the minds of cats.—
"Do birds at dawn *intend* to greet the sun?"

—Pretty damned strong to face, after the dead,
The minds of beasts, and then our mad

Who though not legion are not few,
Who are not dead, are satisfied in small rooms
Or wandering around on barbered lawns
Not far away, or dully gone to bed
With only now and then some troubled dreams.—

"We're close to them, if they're on earth,
Breath by breath,"
Somebody said poetically in bad faith.

TWO

Coldstream Taggart, the College Traveler, Introduces His Country Doctor Friend

Troubled Zenner Doctor Annie loves
The clapboard cottage where she lives alone
Except for Bach and Jesus and her dream
Of working out her faith until she dies
At a ripe old age, she hopes, devoutly prays.

Death, professional familiar,
Is not her friend at Smith Memorial.
She does anxiety, somewhat of fear.
She says at work it closes on her heart
With every diagnosis as she listens—

Or studies ghostly pictures—or draws some blood.
Death stands around the room at every birth
Of every child she brings into the world.
Nothing strikes her like a child's first cry.
She doesn't want the family in the room.

When winter comes she writes to say come down
To spend an afternoon she's not on call.—
She'll play the great baroque and touch on things
About the value of our simple lives.
The winter rain is never simple there.

Last time was Jesus in Jerusalem,
Who knew he'd be afraid to suffer and die,—
And Buddha easing out of every thing,
Sweet and wise but never crucified,—
And how Bach's music is the mind of God,

Atomic particles in all our graves,
Perfect oblivion music from the ground
Made audible and pleasant to the ear.

Coldstream, the College Traveler, Tells of Meeting Toulouse Bergeron, Doctor Annie's Rich and Famous Estranged Husband

1

Her place was like a target for the moon,—
Eight hundred yards away the piney woods,
And then her pasture with some cattle there,
And three great oaks beside her modest house,
Clapboard with a wide porch that takes the rain
When thunderstorms beat toward her from the Gulf,
An acre of Augustine a shade too high,—
All the center of a contemplation.
She's fast asleep inside.
                              We'd had some fun
Into the rising of the summer night,
The rising of a monstrous lovers' moon.

At 3:00 A.M. I went to cut the grass
With her old pushmower she'll never sell,
Reel-type, no motor, friend. You know the kind.

2

You ask was I aware of vanity,
Aware of dangers as I moved along
In nothing but my less than subtle shorts?—
Barefoot and sweating through the flying grass,
Concluding the house was as white as milk or bone,
Recollecting sensuality,—
Jesus and Siddhartha were not there.
I had as poet Leon says, the blue flow.—
Sin's vanity for once was far from me,
Or stood as far away as all those cows.
I labored harmlessly beneath the moon.
Life's short and I was fixing up her lawn.
I'd have that rascal done before the sun.
Love's labor breaks the heart of everyone.

3

The truck lights bounced two hundred yards away,
A V-8 grinding over her rutted road.
I figured some poor soul without a phone
Had come to get some help and medicine.
Doctor Annie does that sort of thing.—

But what it was was a big-time Cadillac,
The gaudy line I'll get when I retire
To write a short lament about the South
As simple as its multiplicity
And poverty and brutal Christian faith.

He rumbled on beneath the falling moon,
Bearing Annie's secret history.
He'd been the golden gentle boy her dreams—
Cotillion Mississippi dreams—had promised.

4

The Cadillac was teal, the man was pale,
Dressed in a Gulf Coast linen suit, and swore
Aloud in something civilized, in Greek.—
I laughed into myself and thought of death,
My own, a tragedy beneath the moon:
Salesman murdered cutting girlfriend's yard.

He shifted toward Biloxi's supple English.
I realized I'd live a little longer.
He cursed Almighty God. He cursed The Sea.
He raged against The Mysteries of Life,
Was terrible, Sebastian shot with arrows
From the stars.
                    I sympathized with one
In major agony. Go easy, man,
I said. I know our Annie's powerful.

5

—She'd have him put aside his wealth,
The football team he owned, the Falcon Jet
He piloted himself. She'd have him poor,
Incapable of generosity,
And she didn't ever want to have his child.

How'd you come to marry her? I wondered.

He said because she hadn't been to school,
Meaning her time at Tulane Medical.
She hadn't taken Gross Anatomy
And hadn't done her time at Charity.
The girl he'd married was a brilliant creature
Capable of joy.
                He's getting a divorce.
He said he'd done more good than Annie had.
I told him Coldstream's only passing through.

6

I'll say he broke apart the night we met.
I'll say the moon was turned to stone for him
The night he found me fooling with her mower.
I told him go inside and talk to her.—
He fetched a little dance and sang to me—
If she won't call my name, I'm gone, I'm gone.

Friend, he backed it on up, turned it around,
As cold as anyone who has to die.

This fellow was your Toulouse Bergeron,
His mother being Greek.
                Years later he
Would not return out of the setting sun,
Flying low toward the Yucatán,
And all of us would feel the cause was Annie,
Though Annie wouldn't tell the press a thing.

7

I finished as the weather covered up
The moon, a steady hour of work or more.
Concatenations with continuous thunder.
I took my coffee on the porch and waited
For Annie to come and tell her version of it,
The which she did in her most flagrant way,
Though quietly. She'd heard our friend Toulouse.

She asked me had I noticed the port wine stain
That covers his right ear, goes down his neck,
Said other stains are scattered across his back,
Said otherwise his body's fairly perfect.
She said I'd never kissed the bister spot
Between her breasts. I said I thought I had.—
A country scene with lovers, lightning, rain!

Coldstream Taggart—
the College Textbook Salesman—
Proposes to His Longtime Friend
Doctor Annie While Listening to Music

A bitter winter Sunday afternoon
In Smith County, Mississippi, and she,
The country doctor, strange and hurt again,
Takes no solace from a reverie
By Brahms, Symphony Number Four. She cries
For all the slaughtered in a recent war.

I say, Play Mozart. Put the dead at ease.
She says, Your single gift is touching fear
The way I would debride a gunshot wound.
I say, Please cut that praise into my stone.

We laugh. I watch her, hand by skillful hand,
Sweeten down to lightest flesh and bone.
I say, Please marry me. She says, I can't.
I want, I say. I want. I want. I want.

Belfontaine, the Star, Removes Himself
from an Unworthy Journalist
and Writes a Song

for Judi Marshall

The fellow wants to do a piece on me,
Which is of course just fine. Fame pays the bills
By drawing crowds, selling records, fills
My heart with pride. I do a better show.

Hell yes, I say, in Jackson at The Inn.
I'll talk for hours, tell about the crime
Of mixing bluegrass up with Cajun music,
Which is my style. Purists call it tragic.

He doesn't know a dobro from a drum,
That's obvious, but still I say come on—
Couldn't tell a fiddle from loose shit.
Poor fucker doesn't have your mother wit.

He says he wants my *personality*—
The secret of my genius with a song.
He's wise into the ways of flattery.
He loved truth once, and then went seriously wrong.

We're on the phone. I say, I'll die like a dog
If I'm unlucky, painfully and thoughtlessly.
He says I'm *entertainment history.*
I say my music is my favorite dog.

Which should have sent him off to somehow write
Whatever he wanted to. He says The Inn
Is not exactly what he had in mind.
He wants to travel with me on my bus.

I say that when the bus begins to move,
It must exclude the ones I do not love.
I say, Please meet me at The Jackson Inn.
I'll sing you where I've been, I'll sing a song.

The Complicated Entertainer
Travis Belfontaine Tells What
Accounts for His Style

My mother says he had our pretty name
And was the brightest guy she'd ever met,
Like a shower of stars, and made her laugh.
Corey Belfontaine.
He worked refineries in Baton Rouge,
And so she married him,
Married how so sweetly he could sing
And play the guitar and the saxophone
He'd picked up growing up in Lafayette.

She says for years we were a family
A girl gets on her knees to ask God for.
For years he was a sweet lighthearted man,
And often I remember him that way,—
Playing—Momma smiling on the porch.
We're singing "All Around the Water Tank,"
"Power in the Blood," that type of thing.—
All this before he made the choice to drink,
Or chose to drink too much.

He made some strange decision in his mind
About the possibilities of life
That ruined everything,
Imagined for their marriage
Curious pleasures she found pitiful.
"I swear I loved him and was satisfied,
And thought he was," she said.
He cursed and hit her for her innocence,
Then left for Baton Rouge forever more.

He left the instruments
And never failed to send his money home,
And wrote us letters for about a year,

Friendly letters. He taught me how to pick.
He taught me how to think,—
And I have never touched a living soul
Who didn't want the touch,
And I know a sober night of ecstasy
Is good and not far from the best there is.

Entertainer Belfontaine
Gets Caught in a Vanity,
Misses an Opportunity to Remain Silent,
and Does More Harm Than Good

Sweetheart, I'm not like anyone you've known.
Nobody's like your father going mad,
Or your troubled husband quickly going bad
On yellow pills and whisky in Des Moines.

Your daddy's schizophrenia was gene
By gene by gene, a destiny, and sad.
Remember him not gone around the bend
In love too much with you. Know what I mean?

Your husband wanted you to be like him?
Wanted you to shave your pretty head?
I'm plain vanilla, as you know, in bed.
Life's stranger, friend, than any dream we dream,

And I'm not inclined to aggravate the plan.
Honey, I've got five daughters, all well grown,
And each has got a mother of her own.
Christ, I'm as sober as a judge, and clean.

I'm not like him or him. I'm neither one.
You say no lover's ever worth the pain?
I'm not expensive and not here for long.
I came in here to love you for a song.

The District Attorney Considers Resignation

for Bob Evans

1
The victim in this case was a white female,
A seventeen-year-old named Johnette Key,
The daughter of my best friends to this day,
Or were, until the months dragged on, until
Nobody was arrested, not a soul
And not a clue.
                    "Johnette will grow a big tree
Before we catch someone," the old men say.

I'm new to mockery. I've done so well
At what I do I'm dying of that child—
Abducted—killed—we pulled out of the creek
All out of shape and ripe about full dark.

It was July and terrible and still
And how she was ought not to have been seen
By her parents, kin, or friends, or anyone,
No matter what's the new psychology.

2
We want a remedy!—
But comes no punishment for what was done.
There's no revenge to satisfy our pain,
And maybe I should resign.—
The torturer has gone to someplace else
As freely as a springtime cloud will pass.

The D.A.'s Prayer

Grant to me a proper hopelessness
That I not be too often alone with joy.—
Such pleasures of my soul are dubious,
O Lord, you know, are measures of the boy

From aunts who set him on a playful throne
Because he was so small. An honest father,
A loving mother make me glib. Atone
The easy patter and the careless banter—

Strike more constantly against my heart
The fact of my mortality. Take back
Considerable of grace, that I repeat,
Without shame, curses honestly. A black
Rage from time to time is what I need
To do good inside this world, and less pride.

A Week in the Life
of the Shy Four-County D.A.
from the Piney Woods

1

A five-day trial, a murderer let off,
Although I did define the murder *rude*.
My final argument was strong enough:
That a scoundrel shoots a man in his own bedroom
Is mortal *rudeness*—viciousness—and wrong.
Which usually works.
              The jury will come to grief
For their decision. He will kill again.
He's pretty as an Elvis imitator
And so they cut him loose. My point of view.
He's trash as crazy as a road lizard.
The defense said there wasn't evidence
Enough. For sure. The evidence is dead.
When a female jury can't be counted on,
The end is near. Sweet sanity is gone.

2

Up to a Jackson party, divorcées
And married ladies out to test their powers.
There was—well cast—a Shakespeare play before,
And I hoped his comedy would bring my way
Some pleasant conversation and a kiss,
A laugh, a scented breast drawn close to mine.
And here she came, striking, Junoesque,
With facts about my faithful years in court,
My bachelorhood, certain persons I've dated,
How I'm—somehow—a country Baptist deacon,
Our rural Kierkegaard. How did she know?
They flee from me that sometime did me seek
Came back to me. Also—*How like you this?*
Her arms were long but O they were not small.

3

She was a Jackson woman in her prime,
Wonderfully alive from stem to stern,
Lay reader, high Episcopalian,
Unmarried at the time. She made that clear

Then asked, What will you do when we're alone?—
You know this has to be? *It was no dream.*
In heels she met me eye to eye at least.
She drew me well aside, then spoke again,
And thoughtfully: When I'm undressing there?

I lit her cigarette. I lit my own.
I said, I'll pray you do a lovely favor.
I'll say continue in your slip awhile.
Only the slip be on. Who knows how long?

She would have voted to convict the man.

After Years of Family
a Local Man's Last Words

I'm not crazy, Leroy. I'm growing wise
Enough to get along alone for years
Maybe. Maybe.
                    Speak of it as vows
I've taken, or say he won't talk because
Some nerve is a wilted flower or blown fuse.

The wife may like the vows reason. God knows?
The children will want to hear of some disease
Having to do with aging.
                    That I choose
To not talk to a blessed soul again
Will cut me off from everyone I love,
But love of course is what did talking in,
Or talking did-in love. They're fine children.

They're making their ways and my bride says I'm mean.

I'll kill your ass, you tell them how I grieve.

A Report—After They're Dead—by Someone Who Knew Both Bob and Sue and Sometimes Wonders Was There Any Hope for Them

1
Bob tried to make sense of the pills she took
And sometimes how she'd drink a quart of gin
Like water down but never stop the pain.—
She'd say she's programmed for her heart to break
And then tell Bob to go on with that talk
About how what she does to him is fun
In bed.—She loved the way he'd grin and groan.

She loved how after sex they'd wash and walk
Out under stars, enjoying all the night
Before the plummet down to worse than bleak,
Where she's a squirrel in the croker sack
Her daddy'd carry from the woods, his hat
Set at a raffish angle, pure delight
And plans for stew to eat.

2
Bob'd smoke while she would swallow one or two
Then rage until she's almost out of breath
About the poverty she'd grown up with.—
Her momma sewing, nothing ever new.—
Her sisters and brothers favored all the time.—
Daddy worthless but for fish and game.—
Bob'd signal how this wasn't entirely true.

I asked her to explain.
Did he beat you? Or whip up on your mom?
She said she lost her one sweet brother, Tom,
In Vietnam. Her eyes were soon a-dream
And satisfied nobody was to blame
For anything.
                    Sue's heart burst soon enough
And Bob's long dying started with a little cough.

That Mobile Lawyer's
Life of Desire

One time on the way to Baton Rouge
I didn't care about the women, Lord,
And that was very good.
I bought a pint of raw oysters in Biloxi
And didn't care about the marriage or
The wrong girl in Birmingham.
The car was paid for, the day was hot
And green off in the trees,
Deciduous and pine,
And I got lost in Tangipahoa,
Or maybe East and West Feliciana.
I studied every motion of the sun
And didn't give a damn.
God knows, I was a fellow with no plan,
A fellow on the run,
But steady all that afternoon until
A serious rain came down.

I found myself a bridge that came to mind
And stopped to smoke and watch a river jump,
Imagined getting on toward Baton Rouge
And maybe a lady in a summer dress,
A lady wearing a complex perfume.
Stepping into some sweet underthing,
She's smiling, moved by possibilities.

Lord, that time again.

The New Orleans Lawyer Describes How a Partner Damaged Himself

You listen to a fellow lie. You know
He's lying. Others in the room do too.
I'll check—and they will check—and find what's true
Is otherwise than his report. What's so

Is the fucking opposite of what he's saying.
This shit is not about to work, so why
Is he continuing? He isn't kidding.
He wants something. He thinks it worth a try.

His wife's like pretty music—high cornet.
She's happy with the noontime and the night,
And they are carrying no heavy debt.
The world's a dream and he is getting caught.

If we're as stupid as he thinks, the thrill
Is his. We lose. He wins if we're asleep.
Outside our windows here, the sky is still,
The city hums, and on the river a ship—

His credibility—moves down the channel.
I tell him, "Friend, Johnny, you've twisted it.
Compadre, we're not fools."
The liar shrugs, abstracted. Comes the vote.

We win a victory for honesty,—
Or playing by Louisiana rules.
The river looks like money in the sun,
And steady power, and a valuable ship is gone.

We're Listening to the Features Editor

1
The bad baby was my secretary's
And she believed that it was mine as well,
For all the reasons of our time together,
But did admit to other company,
Then laughed her laugh and said she knows it's mine,
And all my misery agreed with her.

And, no, she didn't want to see the thing,
Because the nurse said it was incomplete
And dead, anencephalic.

I figured out the word,
A six-month rough draft nature rejected,
And Margie said she'd known I'd want a look.
She'd told the nurse my curiosity,
And that would have to be this afternoon.

2
The nurse, perfection in her every part,
Tall, blue and beautiful
Was down the hall and to the left and right,
Please follow me,
As if I needed all the help I'd get,
And what I got was more than I deserved.

The nurse and I were come into a lab
That was a great deal like a kitchenette.—
She paused at the refrigerator door
To say she'd never seen one born that way,
Eyes wide and the mouth open,
Agape, staring from the perineum,
Face first and dead.
She said remember that it has no brain.

3

She took it from a pinkish baby blanket
With little figures there,
Though I can't remember what the animal,
And placed it nicely on the shining table.

Well, here we are, I thought, and there it is,
With a frightened gargoyle's face (no skull behind)
As terrible as all we fear of error.

Some delicate intestines were spilled out
And I saw the nurse was lightly touching them,
Then so was I
And then I asked her could I hold the baby.

I was amazed to feel its heft and cold,—
As the nurse relaxed while I was studying
No brains, some bowels out, and his pitiful clubbed feet.

THREE

With Tom Royals
I Hope to Visit Gay Ward Atwood's Grave
in Smith County, Mississippi,
Sometime This Summer

That Gay Ward is dead is hard to believe—
As quick a man as ever drew a breath—
But is a fact, and we'll go down to Smith
Before the summer ends to Gay Ward's grave,
And we'll stand there as planned, shaking a fifth
Of Jack Daniels the way he would alive,
Airing it out for silkiness, and grieve,
Drinking it straight, passing it back and forth.

We'll drive to Smith County the way we've done
So many times before through all that green
Of undergrowth and pasturage and pine
And contemplate the difference: Gay's stone
And none of him to say
A cool, remorseless, funny Gay Ward line,
No Gay Ward at the house with Kathryn.

We'll soon be standing on
Some ground that has our friend below,
But I won't guess at what we'll do just then,
Except for whiskey sweat and summer sun
Or average passing clouds or summer rain.

At the Roadhouse He Turns to His Wife with an Observation on Mortality, Then Asks Her for a Dance

By middle age most lose the heart to think,
Go back to being Christians, Jews, or join
Some cult imported from the Orient,—
And I don't mean Zen: Zen's likely some truth
Concerning where we are and what we aren't.

Some of the brightest—once—have their palms read,
Pay cash in Tulsa to a medium,
Death coming to them nightly in a dream
That features ridicule from a severed head.

God knows I know the very one and can't
Say I have never heard the echoing scream—
My own—I've frightened you with at 4:00 A.M.
So, friend, right now let's get out there and dance,
Avoiding fear and local ignorance.

For John Clellon Holmes

Shirley sent this photograph of John
Before the surgeons took his lower jaw
With strategies to put a new one in.
Their lovely plan was pluck out cancer's claw,
Be sure they got it all. They never did.
Next came his tongue, the cancer going on
Into an artery until he died.

Both hands hold tightly to the other one,
Thick hedge behind.
                    Wearing a pale blue robe
With darker piping, he's outside in the sun,
And after all these years I can't describe
His eyes on Shirley.
                    White T-shirt beneath,
Hair combed and shining, he is in some pain.
A Bloody Mary's on the tablecloth.

The True Report about the Day
Garrett Improved His Fellow Poets

George put up with us all afternoon
In odd Spokane, at the Medical Motel,
Across the street from the dying and the ill,
That's where—poets drunk and carrying on.
He told his stories, matching pain for pain,
Orlando to L.A., funny as hell,
Then said, *This calm north light we're playing in
Is secretly about its own sweet will.*

He left the room awhile, then reappeared.
Showered, pink as a babe, wrapped in a towel,
He leapt into the little hall. We cheered.
He was on fire and his violent smile
Refined a place grown suddenly very still.
He said, *It's worse than we have ever imagined.*

Dentistry

I'm reading Zen again, long after noon,
Reading to set aside long thoughts of death,
Trying to be a fifty-year-old man
Who's fairly satisfied no matter what,
The indivisibility of life
And also emptiness of every thing
A satisfaction to my heart and mind,
A satisfaction to *mody* or *bind*,
Whatever one condition we remain.

Because at dawn I lost another tooth
And held it to the light when it was out,
Feeling like Hamlet in the Yorick scene,
My tongue moving toward the bloody socket,
I'm reading Zen again into the night.

He Contemplates
a Further Use of Travel

When next I'm justified to kill someone
And start the suffering because I won't,
And know a year will pass before I'm right,
I'll claim the outrageous *altiplanos* light
Again, and Quechua women with bowlers on.—
I'll think how perfectly their Derbies fit,
Hat by hat, like capitols of felt
Above terrific faces, and I'll be fine.

Justice is one thing, travel another,
And a passport lost is a prime catastrophe.
Who'd miss God's dry, abstract Andean weather?
Who'd risk incarceration in our jail?
High Titicaca'd be impossible
If I took out the ones who trouble me.

He's Living through the Subject of Abortion

Somebody finds one of the guns around
Because we're drinking whisky, playing cards,
Talking art and life out at the lake,
Talking Buddha, Jesus and abortion,
Reason and emotion,—
And you know how that sometimes goes—the sins
Of a lifetime extinguished on the spot,
And then to call his wife, the little plot
Where one of us is buried all too soon,
The powdered face, a wrong about the air
Of grief and general embarrassment.

But it didn't happen.—
Although I said a baby is at sea
Inside or out the womb for a long time
And should be killed with plenty of respect,
If killed at all. Some ritual is called for
While we are practicing infanticide.—
Although a thirty-eight was in my face.—

He cried, "You're the God damned fetus, buddy!"
I took the gun away from a decent steward.—
Outside the lodge I fired all the rounds
Toward the darkness of the water where we are.

Armory Dance—
Some Lines of Boogie and Blues
for Jerry Lee Lewis

The very hardest kind to do
Tells how down at the Armory
Your raunchy songs could make us blue—
To make an old boy see, Lord see
That God damned Armory again
Exactly how it was is mean

But here goes, Jerry Lee, for you
A lovers' verse struck one beat short,
Less elegant but just as true
As any easy bolt heart-shot
Inside the Renaissance. For me
Good buddy, jam it out, go free

Inside the Jackson Armory
Again. Mostly sex. Sex it was—
Sex it was we came to see—
Because because because because
Down at the Armory was where
The sweet girls made damp underwear.

We suffered lovely misery
Down at the Armory to dance—
We held small bodies we could see
Were bopping in a sweaty trance.—
Jerry Lee, that was a hard time,
But after all it was sublime.

It was so fine to run a hand
Down on her back, her tender spine
Until the very end. Again
Again again, God damn the sin
We rubbed down at the Armory.
It was unkind, was misery—

I swear it was, Jerry, I swear
That every hammer of your keys
Made chances better in the car—
We'd finish off between their knees.
We'd bring them off beneath a star.
You showed with music who we are.

Late Summer with Maps and Self-Pity

"Our children go away to other lives,"
Some friends say, "but we're just fine. Are you O.K.?"
I'm neither. I'm the one who always grieves
When they go. I want them here, at work, at play,
At whatever age impossibility affords.

Good God! *To other lives!* I'm immature.
I want them not so far away in beds
I pass while visiting.
                        A rational fear
Of where they are—and they are everywhere—
Has addled me. Jesus. Marrakech.
The Gothic Quarter of Barcelona.
Horrible Turkey. Even two in Bursa.

Bolivia! Now there's a place I like,
A place I've been to, where I'll go again,
My Spanish better, you bet,
About to set out on a river voyage
North toward the Amazon, toward the sea,
Forgetting everything that's troublesome,—
Especially the bodies of everyone I love,—
Especially the detail work of a broken heart.

Postcard from Manaus

At the confluence of the Amazon
And Rio Negro, the famous line was there,
No disappointment, one mighty river brown,
The other black, and O the sweetest air
In all the world. Happy. Wish you were here.
Some days it's hard to realize you're there.—
And then we heard the clearest cries. Not fear
Exactly. Though maybe over water fear
Is different, the way it carries a name.

Voices were blazing in the midday sun—
Because one of the little boats that work
The rivers had lost a child, the yelling so near
To where we were the trick was not to think
He's safe enough—the rivers won't take him down.
His people in the water rescued him.
Then Carnival! Iquitos to Belém!
God almighty, what a place to drown
Came straight to mind. I'll soon be coming home.

He Becomes Corrosive While Thinking about the Pope's Recent Sermons to the Poor of Latin America

The Pope's a busy guy, be sure of that,
Whether he's grey and pretty without his hat,
Or obviously out of date with the damned thing on,—
Too busy to have a vision based on reason,—
The Reasonable Vision of the Holy Condom,
The Holy Foam, the Holy Pill or Shot,
Whatever he might say is God's sweet will.
The Pope's a bad poet and his prose is cruel.

He's a killer when it comes to words.
Look at his face. He doesn't look like sin.
The devil's a gentleman.—A flight of birds
Off a dead child explains this father's rule.
Worms from a mother's eyes are how he does
God's will. Sometimes he seems a lord of flies.

On the Hall of the Oncology Floor

for Gary Wilson, 1954–1982

His doctor says that Gary's soul is lost
And about to go to hell eternally
Unless he accepts the Lord Jesus Christ.—
He's speaking to me very levelly
Without compassion in his Baptist eyes,
Says he's told Gary several times to choose
Heaven. Hurry accept God's sacrifice,
Accept the living gospel, the good news.

Gary Wilson is dying in his room,
Scared of oblivion, but not inclined
To buy into a surgeon's insane dream
Of endless pain.
                    Gary's a rational man,
Scholar, artist, linguist, constant friend.
Surely—surely there's something to be learned.

Face the Nation: One from State

I'll have to say his face is generous—
In fact I'll bet his Sunday drink is orange juice
With gin in it, like mine sometimes. He's calm loose
On the T.V. and likes the world and us.

No doubt it's true his face is not quite blessed.—
It is rather fallen like creation, a truce
Being the best it can imagine, a fierce
Desire for nicer foreigners for us

To deal with over orange juice and gin
On Sunday mornings. He's not bad at all,
Even though Republican. His peace
Of mind cannot define a term like sin
Or anything that's not political,
But maybe Christ were nicer as gin and orange juice.

A Poem for My Humerus

1
A recent x-ray of my arm and shoulder
Set me against cremation's cleansing fire
More than I was before.
One time I heard it called *a cleansing fire*,
Suggesting guilt and terrible regret
Concerning life on earth. I'm not for that.—
Also, one time I called to ask about
A funeral, was told that the cremains
Were at the home of the deceased.
                                        Say what?
There'd be a service in another city.
Cremains! O this is how the language dies
Or says we're desperate for metaphor
To give a little dignity to death,
A sort of mousse with ashes that won't do.

2
My humerus was lovely glowing there
Upon the wall, looking like the moon,
Or at least its head did, lit from behind,
The doctor smiling over my old wounds,
Scores in the bone, stray pieces of calcium.—
Worst comes to worst, he said, we'll take it out—
My humerus!—and put a new one in
Made from incredible materials.

I asked him could I have the one displaced.
I realized I'd want it in a case
On view, with a bright plaque explaining things
The arm had done, helped by its hand,—tackles,
Blocks, embraces, many sentences.—
But it won't come to that, the doctor said.

3

Some Christians won't cremate because they fear
Much difficulty with the resurrection,
God finding problems with the chemistry
It takes to put a body back together
After fire.
       I'm not concerned with that,
For—alas—the Christian reconstruction
Seems far-fetched, to say the very least,
And is a mighty viciousness when faith
That some will rise tortures all the others.
Tacky or *vicious* seems to be the word.

Christ, I'd be rendered to a skeleton,
Then let an archeologist come on.
She's fascinated. She is taking notes.
She holds my humerus up to the sun.

For My Father at Eighty

For years he never talked about the war
Except to name some places he had been,
Le Havre, Remagen, moving on Berlin.
I wanted him to tell some outright fear

He'd suffered in his bravery, the roar
Of German eighty-eights, the flinch of pain,
The dead, some hatred, a severe *God damn.*
For years he kept his peace, and he's never sworn.

Mother told me not to trouble him.
Maybe or not he'll somehow find the time,
And if he does, then leave the man alone.
You've no idea what the man has seen.

One afternoon, when I was married, grown,
A good time in the best of company,
He joined our easy talk of history.
Miller and Ward and Gen were there. He'd seen

The armies' soldiers, frozen, torn apart,
And, worse, a death camp, thousands naked and starved,
In five great pits, enough to break your heart.
We did our best. Only three survived.

His story was five hundred words, no more.
He told it well. He'd told his war.
My father's a gentle Presbyterian.
At eighty, thoughtful, he believes in hell.